Highlights

The ULTIMATE EMOJI Puzzle Book

HIGHLIGHTS PRESS
Honesdale, Pennsylvania

Face to Face

Across the Farm

It's time to head in for the night. Can you find the right path across the farm? The emojis will tell you which way to move.

 Move 1 space RIGHT

 Move 1 space DOWN

 UP Move 1 space

 Move 1 space LEFT

PATH 1	PATH 2	PATH 3	PATH 4	PATH 5	PATH 6
tractor	corn	corn	corn	tractor	corn
tractor	corn	corn	tractor	corn	corn
cow	pig	pig	corn	pig	corn
corn	corn	pig	pig	tractor	corn
tractor	tractor	corn	corn	cow	tractor

EXIT

 for Answers

There are 29 different fish words and phrases hidden in this grid. For each one, the word FISH has been replaced by . Look up, down, across, backwards, and diagonally.

WORD LIST

- ANGELFISH
- ARCHERFISH
- BLOWFISH
- BLUEFISH
- BONEFISH
- BUTTERFISH
- CATFISH
- CRAYFISH
- CUTTLEFISH
- DOGFISH
- FISHBOWL
- FISHERMAN
- FISH-EYE
- FISHHOOK
- FISHTAIL
- FLYING FISH
- GOLDFISH
- JELLYFISH
- KINGFISH
- NOODLE FISH
- PARROT FISH
- RIBBONFISH
- SCORPION FISH
- SHELLFISH
- STARFISH
- SUNFISH
- SWORDFISH
- TRIGGERFISH
- ZEBRA FISH

B	U	T	T	E	R	🐟	G	G	O	L	D	🐟
O	L	🐟	E	L	T	T	U	C	L	D	N	D
F	I	E	P	A	R	R	O	T	🐟	O	I	R
F	A	R	C	H	E	R	🐟	S	I	🐟	H	O
L	T	M	H	A	I	R	C	P	H	🐟	L	W
Y	🐟	A	V	B	E	R	R	O	E	W	🐟	S
I	E	N	B	G	A	O	O	N	O	T	E	U
N	W	O	G	Y	C	K	O	B	E	O	U	N
G	N	I	🐟	S	T	B	🐟	Y	E	E	L	🐟
🐟	R	D	O	G	🐟	L	E	G	N	A	B	R
T	T	B	L	O	W	🐟	Y	L	L	E	J	A
K	I	N	G	🐟	Z	E	B	R	A	🐟	H	T
S	H	E	L	L	🐟	E	L	D	O	O	N	S

TRIVIA QUESTION:

What do goldfish have in the back of their throat?

Put the uncircled letters in order on the blanks.

— — — — — — — — — — — — — — —

— — — — —!

Trouble

The letters C-A-R are the start of a load of words. Use the clues to help figure out the rest of each word.

1. Send one of these for birthdays or holidays: ____

2. To slice turkey or make figures of wood: ____ ____

3. Milk container: ____ ____ ____

4. A rug: ____ ____ ____

5. Orange vegetable that grows in the ground: ____ ____ ____

6. Comic strip: ____ ____ ____ ____

7. Relative of moose and elk: ____ ____ ____ ____

8. Chewy candy: ____ ____ ____ ____

9. Red bird: ____ ____ ____ ____ ____

10. A fair: ____ ____ ____ ____ ____

11. A flower that blooms in many colors: ____ ____ ____ ____ ____ ____

12. Sideways handspring with a twist: ____ ____ ____ ____ ____ ____

13. Meat eater: ____ ____ ____ ____ ____ ____

14. Capital of Nevada: ____ ____ ____   ____ ____ ____

In All Weather

Every type of weather should only appear once in each row, column, and 2 x 3 box. Fill in the squares by drawing or writing the name of each weather type.

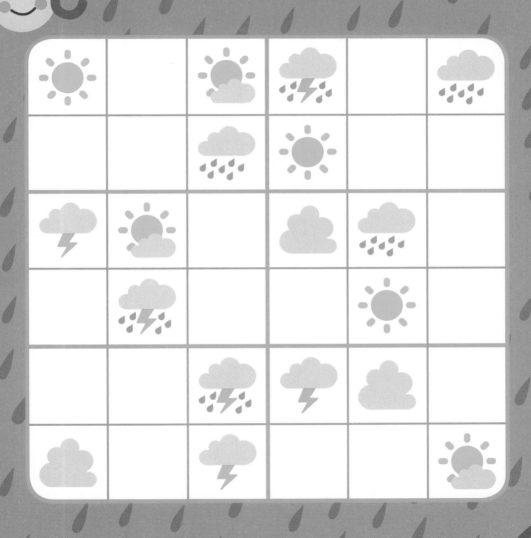

Amusing Animals

There are five animal jokes on the next page. Use the emoji code to fill in the letters and finish the jokes. Then tell them to your friends!

Emoji Code

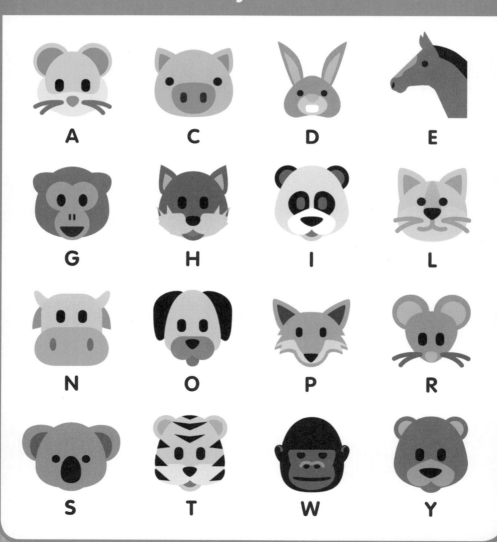

A

C

D

E

G

H

I

L

N

O

P

R

S

T

W

Y

Where do horses go when they're sick?

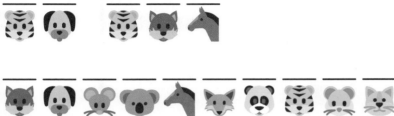

_____ _____   _____ _____ _____

What does a bear call its grandfather?

_____ _____ _____ _____ _____ - _____ _____ _____

What dog can tell time?

_____   _____ _____ _____ _____ _____   _____ _____ _____

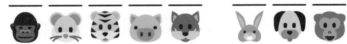

How does a hog write a letter?

_____ _____ _____ _____   _____   _____ _____ _____ _____ _____ _____

What kind of kitties like to go bowling?

_____ _____ _____ _____ _____   _____ _____ _____ _____

Taking

Circle sets of four emojis together that have one of each instrument. One side of each square must touch a side of another square in the same set. You are done when all the squares are circled.

Give 'Em a Taste

Can you complete each common phrase with the correct emoji?

The _____ of my eye

A couch _____

Don't cry over spilled _____

One smart _____

When life gives you _____

Don't put all your _____ in one basket

Bigger _____ to fry

The big _____

Easy as _____

Best thing since sliced _____

Two-Faced Match

Each emoji face but one has an exact match. Can you find the one without a match?

Countdown

Find: 5 ♥ 4 😜 3 ☂ 2 🐨 1 ✌

Here Comes the ☀

There are 29 different sun words hidden in this grid. For each one, the word SUN has been replaced with ☀. Look up, down, across, backwards, and diagonally.

WORD LIST

SUNBAKED
SUNBATHE
SUNBEAM
SUNBLOCK
SUNBURN
SUNBURNED
SUNDAE
SUNDAY
SUNDECK
SUNDIAL
SUNDOWN
SUNDRESS
SUNFISH
SUNKEN
SUNLIGHT
SUNLIT
SUNNIER
SUNNY
SUNRAY
SUNRISE
SUNROOF
SUNROOM
SUNSCREEN
SUNSET
SUNSHINE
SUNSPOT
SUNTAN
TSUNAMI
UNSUNG

```
☀ L I G H T O P S ☀ T ☀
☀ H H E S K I Z R ☀ N B
B S R E C I E O B ☀ E E
A I L E M N O U N B K A
K F D A I M R O E U ☀ M
E ☀ ☀ H I N S S E R D ☀
D T S Y E D ☀ F R N T ☀
A ☀ A D Y N ☀ U C E I R
☀ R O O F N D N S ☀ L I
☀ B L O C K A ☀ ☀ T ☀ S
I ☀ B A T H E G C A K E
☀ D O W N ☀ D A Y N E L
```

TRIVIA QUESTION:

If the sun was the size of a door in your house, how big would Earth be?

Put the uncircled letters in order on the blanks.

___ ___ ___ ___   ___ ___ ___ ___ ___   ___ ___   ___   ___ ___ ___ ___ ___ ___

Pizza and ice cream are the perfect pair for this pair of mazes. From START to FINISH, pass through all of the emojis, alternating between pizza and ice cream. You may not retrace or cross your path.

1 for All

The letters O-N-E are part of a lot of words.
Use the clues to help figure out the rest of each word.

1. Ice-cream holder: __ 🏅

2. Finished: __ 🏅

3. Skeleton part: __ 🏅

4. Sticky sweetener made out of nectar by bees: __ 🏅 __

5. Coins and bills: __ 🏅 __

6. By yourself: __ __ 🏅

7. British pastry, eaten with clotted cream and jam: __ __ 🏅

8. Sticks and _____: __ __ 🏅 __

9. A giant, rotating storm: __ __ __ __ 🏅

10. Use this to call someone: __ __ 🏅

11. Not here anymore: __ 🏅

12. Musical instrument played with mallets: __ __ __ __ __ __ 🏅

13. King's chair: __ __ __ 🏅

14. Truthful: __ 🏅 __ __

Just Wing It

Every type of bird should only appear once in each row, column, and 2 x 3 box. Fill in the squares by drawing or writing the name of each bird.

Funny Flora

There are five plant jokes on the next page. Use the emoji code to fill in the letters and finish the jokes. Then tell them to your friends!

Emoji Code

A	**B**	**D**	**E**
F	**H**	**I**	**K**
L	**M**	**O**	**P**
R	**S**	**T**	**U**
V	**W**	**Y**	**Z**

What do plants like to drink?

What plant loves math?

What do you call a tree robber?

What did the big flower say to the little flower?

" ___ ___ , ___ ___ ___ . "

What flower does everyone have?

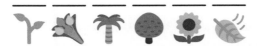

At the Movies

Each movie theater snack costs a different dollar amount. The totals for all four snacks across each row and down each column are noted. It's up to you to find the cost of each snack. Popcorn is $8.00. Start with the bottom row.

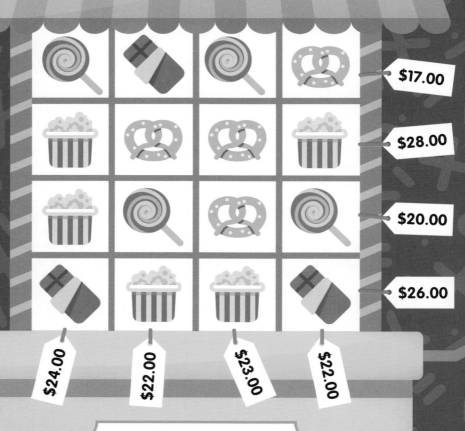

$17.00

$28.00

$20.00

$26.00

$24.00

$22.00

$23.00

$22.00

 = $8.00   = _____

 = _____   = _____

Match 'Em Up

Can you complete each common phrase with the correct emoji?

_____ on thin ice

Once in a blue _____

Music to my _____

Like a kid in a _____ store

As right as _____

An open _____

Every _____ has a silver lining

Sick as a _____

The way the _____ crumbles

An early _____

Find the Faces

Two of these columns have all the same emojis.
Can you find which two columns?

Bonus!
Which emoji appears
in every column?

Just Add Words

Match one emoji with one word to make a compound word. The emoji can go before or after the word. Some emojis have more than one single match, but there is only one solution that creates 10 compound words. We started you off with SUNFISH.

worm

wild

sweet

green

place

under

pop

back

sun

glasses

1. **SUNFISH** _____
2. _____
3. _____
4. _____
5. _____

6. _____
7. _____
8. _____
9. _____
10. _____

25

Make a Move

Compare these two pages. Can you find at least 20 differences?

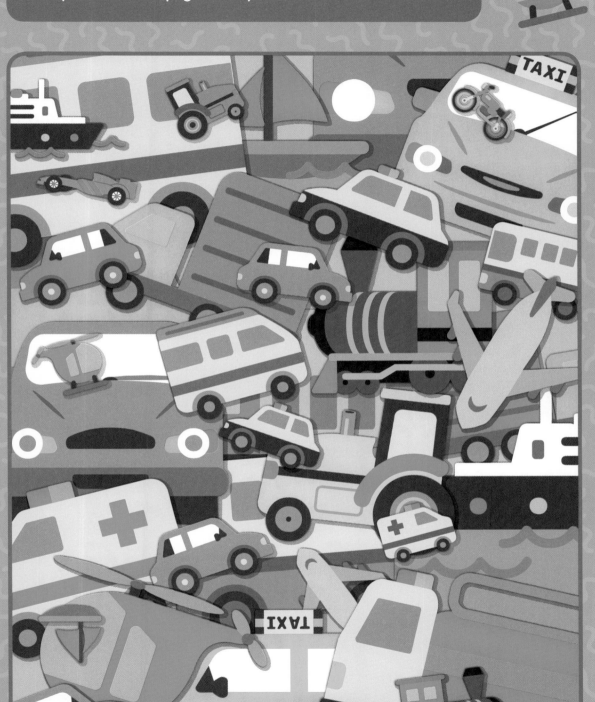

Shot on Goal

The game is almost over. Can you find the right path to score the game-winning goal? The emojis will tell you which way to move.

Move 1 space — RIGHT

Move 1 space — DOWN

UP — Move 1 space

LEFT — Move 1 space

PATH 1	PATH 2	PATH 3	PATH 4	PATH 5	PATH 6

EXIT

On Your 👣

There are 29 different foot words and phrases hidden in this grid. For each one, the word FOOT has been replaced with 👣. Look up, down, across, backwards, and diagonally.

WORD LIST

- BAREFOOT
- BEST FOOT FORWARD
- BIGFOOT
- CROWFOOT
- FLATFOOT
- FOOT FAULT
- FOOT THE BILL
- FOOTBALL
- FOOTBATH
- FOOTBRIDGE
- FOOTGEAR
- FOOTHILL
- FOOTHOLD
- FOOTLIGHT
- FOOTLOCKER
- FOOTLOOSE
- FOOTMAN
- FOOTNOTE
- FOOTPATH
- FOOTPRINT
- FOOTRACE
- FOOTREST
- FOOTSTEP
- FOOTSTOOL
- FOOTWORK
- HOTFOOT
- SURE-FOOTED
- TENDERFOOT
- UNDERFOOT

👣	T	H	E	D	👣	F	A	U	L	T	👣	B
T	S	L	P	L	L	L	I	H	👣	E	L	E
N	E	T	L	👣	L	O	T	R	E	N	O	S
I	R	F	O	I	L	A	H	E	👣	D	O	T
R	👣	R	👣	O	B	O	B	👣	N	E	S	👣
P	E	T	S	👣	L	E	C	O	R	E	F
👣	O	👣	P	A	T	H	H	K	T	👣	S	O
H	T	O	👣	W	O	R	C	T	E	👣	👣	R
R	G	M	U	N	D	E	R	👣	👣	R	W	W
O	A	B	A	👣	L	I	G	H	T	A	O	A
N	R	E	👣	B	R	I	D	G	E	C	R	R
E	F	O	G	O	B	A	R	E	👣	E	K	D
S	U	R	E	👣	E	D	F	L	A	T	👣	T

RIDDLE:

Why doesn't a bear wear socks?

Put the uncircled letters in order on the blanks.

__ __   _____   ___   ___

_____ .

Earn Your

The letters C-O-R-N are part of a lot of words.
Use the clues to help figure out the rest of each word.

1.   Nut from an oak tree: __ 🌽

2.   Where two walls meet: 🌽 __ __

3.   Movie snack: __ __ __ 🌽

4.   A storybook horse with one horn: __ __ __ 🌽

5.   A breakfast cereal: 🌽 __ __ __ __ __ __

6.   Ingredient used for thickening: 🌽 __ __ __ __ __ __

7.   The front layer of the eye: 🌽 __ __

8.   A brass instrument: 🌽 __ __

9.   Crushed and used as a spice: __ __ __ __ __ __ 🌽

10. Food that goes well with soups: 🌽 __ __ __ __ __

11. Horn-shaped container filled with produce: 🌽 __ __ __ __ __ __

12. Funny in a cheesy way: 🌽 __

13. A traditional hair style: 🌽 __ __ __ __

14. A coarse flour: 🌽 __ __ __ __

Face-Off

Every face emoji should only appear once in each row, column, and 2 x 3 box. Fill in the squares by drawing or writing the name of each emoji.

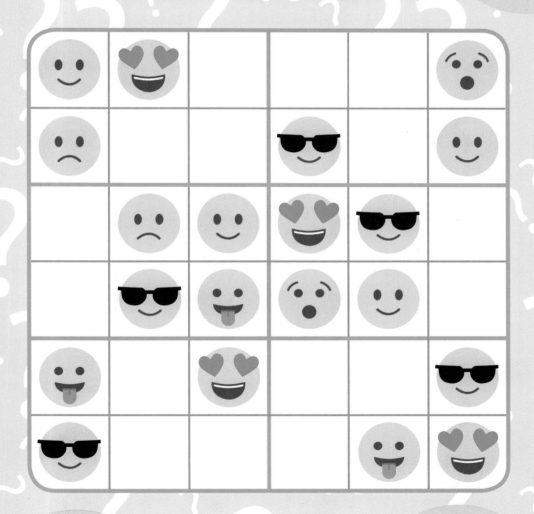

Food Fill-Up

There are four food jokes on the next page. Use the emoji code to fill in the letters and finish the jokes. Then tell them to your friends!

Emoji Code

A	B	C	E
F	H	I	K
L	M	O	P
R	S	T	U
V	W	Y	Z

Why did the cookie see a doctor?

_ _ _ - _ _ .

How do you make an egg roll?

What did the mustard say during the race?

"

 "

How do you fix a broken pizza?

It's Raining and

Circle sets of four emojis together that have two cats and two dogs. One side of each square must touch a side of another square in the same set. You are done when all the squares are circled.

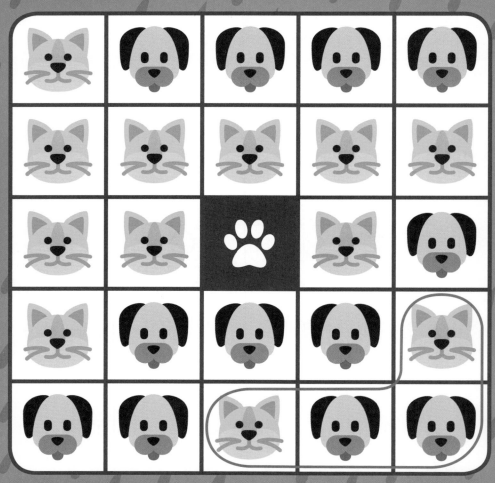

Knock 'Em Out

Can you complete each common phrase with the correct emoji?

Hit the _____

_____ of a feather

In the same _____

Play it by _____

Change of _____

Give someone a _____

Don't cry _____

Get a _____ in the door

I could eat a _____

Barking up the wrong _____

In Good Hands

Each emoji but one has an exact match. Can you find the one without a match?

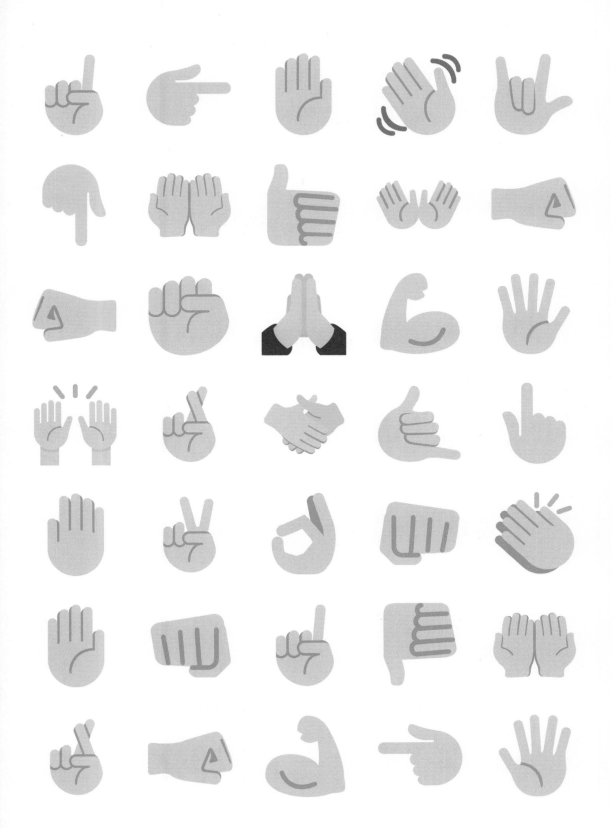

Countdown

Find: 5 😄 4 🐸 3 ➶ 2 🏐 1 😍

Where the ♥ Is

There are 24 different heart words and phrases hidden in this grid.
For each one, the word HEART has been replaced with ♥.
Look up, down, across, backwards, and diagonally.

WORD LIST

BROKENHEARTED
CHANGE OF HEART
CHICKENHEARTED
COLDHEARTED
HALF-HEARTED
HARD-HEARTED
HAVE A HEART
HEART AND SOUL
HEART OF GOLD
HEART OF STONE
HEART TO HEART
HEARTACHE
HEARTBEAT
HEARTBREAK
HEARTBURN
HEARTFELT
HEARTSICK
HEARTTHROB
HEARTWORM
KINDHEARTED
KNOW BY HEART
SWEETHEART
TENDERHEARTED
YOUNG AT HEART

```
♥  O  F  G  O  L  D  E  H  C  A  ♥  ♥
E  N  O  T  S  F  O  ♥  Y  O  U  T  R
D  E  ♥  N  E  K  O  R  B  T  E  A  H
K  C  H  I  C  K  E  N  ♥  E  D  G  E
I  H  ♥  T  H  R  O  B  W  N  A  N  ♥
N  A  M  B  A  R  R  S  ♥  D  D  U  F
D  R  R  T  U  E  H  Y  I  E  E  O  O
♥  D  O  K  A  R  B  A  S  R  ♥  Y  E
E  ♥  W  K  C  W  N  ♥  V  ♥  F  O  G
D  E  ♥  ♥  O  I  N  ♥  F  E  L  T  N
E  D  T  N  G  I  S  A  N  D  A  T  A
P  O  K  C  O  L  D  ♥  E  D  H  ♥  H
♥  U  M  P  ♥  A  N  D  S  O  U  L  C
```

TRIVIA QUESTION:

**The heart is an important organ in our bodies.
It's also something else. What is it?**

Put the uncircled letters in order on the blanks.

_ _ _ _ _   _ _ _ _ _   _ _

_ _ _ _   _ _ _ _ _ _   _ _ _ _ .

39

Maze

Each flower is worth 1, 2, or 3 points as shown on the key.
Can you find a path to pick exactly 37 points worth of flowers?

Key
= 1 point
= 2 points
= 3 points

FINISH

s in Your P🕷s

The letters A-N-T are part of a lot of words.
Use the clues to help figure out the rest of each word.

1. Huge person: __ __ 🕷

2. Animal with a trunk: __ __ __ __ __ 🕷

3. Person who rents an apartment: __ __ __ 🕷

4. Deer horn: 🕷 __ __ __

5. National song: 🕷 __ __ __

6. Kind of flag: __ __ __ __ 🕷

7. Butler or maid: __ __ __ __ 🕷

8. An insect's feeler: 🕷 __ __ __ __

9. A friendly disposition: __ __ __ __ __ 🕷

10. Old, valuable stuff: 🕷 __ __ __ __ __

11. Baby: __ __ __ 🕷

12. A place to store food: __ 🕷 __ __

13. Shelf above a fireplace: __ 🕷 __ __

14. Used to get water when putting out fires: __ __ __ __ 🕷

Snack Break

Every food should only appear once in each row, column, and 2 x 3 box. Fill in the squares by drawing or writing the name of each food.

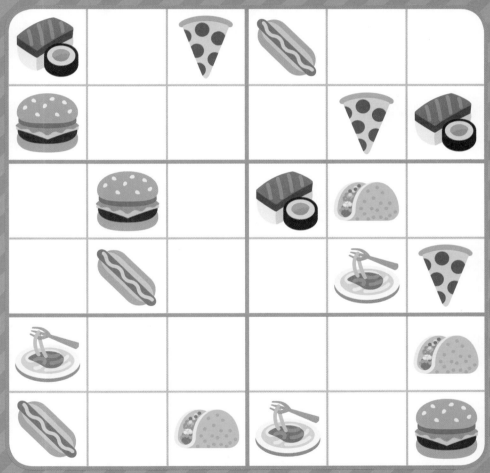

Music Madness

There are four music jokes on the next page. Use the emoji code to fill in the letters and finish the jokes. Then tell them to your friends!

Emoji Code

A	B	E	H
L	M	N	O
P	R	S	T
U	W	Y	Z

What kind of music do mummies like?

What is a bubble's least favorite type of music?

___ ___ ___!

What does a skeleton use to make music?

___ ___ ___ ___ - ___ ___ ___ ___

What do you get when a musician loses their beat?

___ ___ ___ ___ ___ - ___ ___ ___ ___ ___ ___ ___

Where do snowmen dance?

___ ___ ___ ___ ___ ___ ___

Face Value

Each emoji on this page goes with one number. No two emojis have the same number. Can you figure out which number goes with each emoji? The number 7 goes with the emoji wearing sunglasses. Use the equations to figure out the rest.

A + = 12    – = 6

___

B + = 17   –  = 3

___ 7   ___ 7

C + = 14   – = 2

___

D +  = 20   – = 12

___ ___

E + = 13   – = 3

___ ___ ___ ___

F + = 18   – = 4

___ 7   ___ 7

Pack 'Em In

Can you complete each common phrase with the correct emoji?

As white as _____

Over the _____

Off on the wrong _____

That _____ has sailed

On _____ nine

_____ in your stomach

Wear your _____ on your sleeve

_____ of thought

Fit as a _____

Add fuel to the _____

Animal Antics

Two of these columns have all the same emojis.
Can you find which two columns?

Bonus!
Which emoji appears
in every column?

Stick Together

Each of these words is part of two other words. Can you use your stickers to make those two words? For example, take the word SHELL. A sticker in front can make EGGSHELL. A sticker behind it makes SHELLFISH. After you add stickers to that one, see if you can figure out the others.

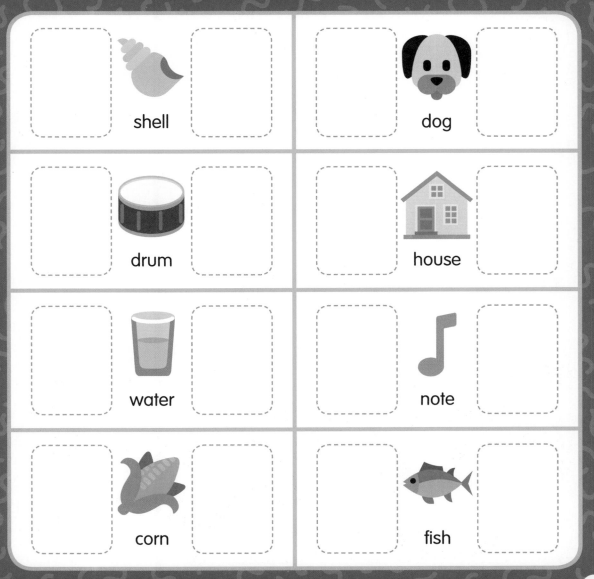

shell

dog

drum

house

water

note

corn

fish

Taste Test

Rainforest Run

The sun is coming out! Can you find the right path through the rainforest to see the rainbow? The emojis will tell you which way to move.

😺ch the Answers

There are 26 different cat words hidden in this grid. For each one, the word CAT has been replaced with 😸. Look up, down, across, backwards, and diagonally.

WORD LIST

- BOBCAT
- CATALOG
- CATAMARAN
- CATBIRD
- CATCHY
- CATEGORY
- CATERPILLAR
- CATFISH
- CATHEDRAL
- CATNAP
- CATNIP
- CATTAIL
- CATTLE
- CATWALK
- COMMUNICATE
- COPYCAT
- DECATHLON
- DEDICATE
- DOGCATCHER
- EDUCATION
- LOCATE
- MULTIPLICATION
- SCATTERED
- TOMCAT
- VACATION
- WILDCAT

D	O	G	😸	C	H	E	R	C	A	😸	M	Y
D	T	D	D	W	T	O	M	😸	S	T	U	H
E	E	C	E	R	A	S	D	C	😸	A	L	C
😸	😸	R	O	D	I	L	A	😸	T	I	T	😸
H	O	A	N	M	I	B	K	Y	E	L	I	N
L	L	L	A	W	M	😸	😸	P	R	T	P	E
O	T	L	R	A	P	U	E	O	E	S	L	E
N	😸	I	A	😸	T	A	N	C	D	T	I	D
E	F	P	M	E	S	😸	N	I	😸	W	😸	U
P	I	R	A	G	B	E	E	😸	😸	T	I	😸
I	S	E	😸	O	😸	A	L	O	G	E	O	I
N	H	😸	B	R	N	V	A	😸	I	O	N	O
😸	E	S	S	Y	L	A	R	D	E	H	😸	N

TRIVIA QUESTION:

What taste are cats unable to detect?

Put the uncircled letters in order on the blanks.

_ _ _ _ _   _ _ _ ' _   _ _ _ _ _

_ _ _ _ _ _ _ _ _ _ _.

I'm All 👂s

The letters E-A-R are part of an 👂ful of words.
Use the clues to help figure out the rest of each word.

1. Usually 365 days long: __ 👂

2. A fruit: __ 👂

3. Make your own money: 👂 __

4. Not cloudy: __ __ 👂

5. A planet: 👂 __ __

6. Not late: 👂 __ __

7. Gain knowledge about something: __ 👂 __

8. Valentine symbol: __ 👂 __

9. Piece of jewelry: 👂 __ __ __ __

10. Not afraid: __ 👂 __ __ __ __

11. These might fall when you're sad: __ 👂 __ __ __ __ __

12. Vanish: __ __ __ __ __ __ 👂

13. What goes on before your clothes: __ __ __ __ __ __ 👂

14. Closeby: __ 👂

Sweet Treat

Every treat should only appear once in each row, column, and 2 x 3 box. Fill in the squares by drawing or writing the name of each treat.

Sports Sillies

There are four sports jokes on the next page. Use the emoji code to fill in the letters and finish the jokes. Then tell them to your friends!

Emoji Code

A

B

C

D

E

F

H

I

L

N

O

R

S

T

U

Y

What did the mitt say to the baseball?

"   "

   ."

What did the two strings do during the race?

          .

Why did it get hot after the soccer game?

          .

What can you serve but not eat?

Why don't fish play basketball?

'

       .

It's No  Matter

Circle sets of four emojis together that have two crying-laughing faces and two wacky faces. One side of each square must touch a side of another square in the same set. You are done when all the squares are circled.

Make 'Em Wild

Can you complete each common phrase with the correct emoji?

Sly as a _____

_____ out of water

Hold your _____

_____ business

A little _____ told me

Let the _____ out of the bag

Night _____

When _____ fly

Can't teach an old _____ new tricks

Quiet as a _____

Puzzling Plants

Each plant emoji but one has an exact match. Can you find the one without a match?

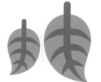

Countdown

Find: 5 🐬 4 🌿 3 😊 2 🚲 1 🍃

Don't Around

There are 27 different horse words and phrases hidden in this grid. For each one, the word HORSE has been replaced with 🐴. Look up, down, across, backwards, and diagonally.

WORD LIST

CLOTHESHORSE
DARK HORSE
EAT LIKE A HORSE
HOBBYHORSE
HOLD YOUR HORSES
HORSEBACK
HORSEFLY
HORSEHAIR
HORSELAUGH
HORSEMANSHIP
HORSEPLAY
HORSEPOWER
HORSERADISH
HORSESHOE
HORSETAIL
HORSEWHIP
HORSE RACE
RACEHORSE
ONE HORSE TOWN
PACKHORSE
ROCKING HORSE
SAWHORSE
SEAHORSE
STRONG AS A HORSE
TROJAN HORSE
WARHORSE
WORKHORSE

H	E	R	🐴	W	A	E	H	L	S	P	J	H
🐴	W	A	S	S	C	🐴	I	G	I	U	O	O
S	🐴	C	P	A	E	A	S	H	U	N	T	B
H	A	E	R	I	T	H	S	H	E	A	A	B
🐴	S	🐴	L	🐴	H	N	T	🐴	O	🐴	L	Y
A	A	I	🐴	R	A	W	T	O	G	E	🐴	🐴
E	G	W	D	M	E	O	🐴	N	L	A	K	I
K	N	O	🐴	A	W	W	I	T	E	C	T	L
I	O	R	F	N	R	K	O	S	A	E	H	🐴
L	R	K	L	O	C	🐴	🐴	P	L	A	Y	H
T	T	🐴	Y	O	D	A	R	K	🐴	R	S	A
A	S	🐴	R	U	O	Y	D	L	O	H	E	I
E	T	R	O	J	A	N	🐴	B	A	C	K	R

RIDDLE:

Why did the pony have to gargle?
Put the uncircled letters in order on the blanks.

__ __   __ __ __ __   __ __ __ __   __

__ __ __ __ __ __ __ __   __ __ __ __ __.

63

START

To go from this maze's cloudy START to its sunny FINISH, you have to find the one path that takes you through alternating clouds and suns. You may not retrace or cross your path.

FINISH

Do!

The letters C-A-N are part of a lot of words.
Use the clues to help figure out the rest of each word.

1. A narrow boat propelled by paddles: C__ __

2. A type of nut: __ __ CAN

3. An artist might paint on this: C__ __ __

4. It lights up a birthday cake, one for each year: C__ __ __

5. Empty, unoccupied: __ __ C__

6. A yellow pet bird: C__ __ __

7. A tropical bird with a colorful beak: __ __ __ C

8. Lava pours out of this: __ __ __ C__

9. A giant rain and windstorm: __ __ __ __ __ C__

10. It can copy images to a computer: __ C__ __ __

11. A sweet treat: C__ __

12. A cover overhead, like fabric over a bed: C__ __ __ __

13. Another word for dog: C__ __ __

14. A melon: C__ __ __ __ __ __ __ __

At the Beach

Every beach emoji should only appear once in each row, column, and 2 x 3 box. Fill in the squares by drawing or writing the name of each emoji.

Emoji Emotions

There are four jokes on the next page. Use the emoji face code to fill in the letters and finish the jokes. Then tell them to your friends!

Emoji Code

A

D

E

F

H

I

M

N

O

P

R

S

T

U

W

Y

Why was the rabbit so happy?

_____ _____ _____   _____ _____ _____   _____

_____ _____ _____ - _____ _____ _____ _____ _____ _____ .

How do clowns like their eggs?

_____ - _____

Why did Sandra cry on February 29th?

_____ _____   _____ _____ _____   _____   _____ _____ _____ _____

_____ _____ _____ _____ .

Why was the dog sad?

_____ _____   _____ _____ _____ _____

_____ _____ _____ _____   _____ _____ _____ .

Animal Addition

Each animal emoji on this page has a value from 1 to 9. No two animals have the same value. Can you use the equations to figure out which number goes with which animal? The frog has the largest number and the rabbit has the smallest number.

Add 'Em Up

Can you complete each common phrase with the correct emoji?

'Til the _____ come home

Piece of _____

Head in the _____

Blind as a _____

Take a _____ check

Costs an _____ and a leg

_____ for a compliment

If the _____ fits

_____ got your tongue

Comparing apples and _____

Transportation Combinations

 Two of these columns have all the same emojis. Can you find which two columns?

 Bonus! Which emoji appears in every column?

Just Add Words

Match one emoji with one word to make a compound word. The emoji can go before or after the word. Some emojis have more than one single match, but there is only one solution that creates 10 compound words. We started you off with BATBOY.

radish

chair

go

boy

shell

light

lace

honey

web

friend

1. **BATBOY**
2. _____
3. _____
4. _____
5. _____

6. _____
7. _____
8. _____
9. _____
10. _____

Wild Web

Smiles for Days

It's one happy day! Can you find the right path through the smiles? The emojis will tell you which way to move.

Move 1 space — **RIGHT**

Move 1 space — **DOWN**

Move 1 space — **UP**

Move 1 space — **LEFT**

PATH 1	PATH 2	PATH 3	PATH 4	PATH 5	PATH 6
😄	😄	😄	😄	😄	😄
😄	😎	😄	😍	😄	😄
😄	🙃	😄	😄	😍	😄
😄	😎	😍	🙃	😄	🙃
😎	🙃	😄	😍	😍	😎

EXIT

Reach for the

There are 30 different star words and phrases hidden in this grid. For each one, the word STAR has been replaced with ★. Look up, down, across, backwards, and diagonally.

WORD LIST

- CORNSTARCH
- CUSTARD
- DASTARDLY
- KICK-START
- LODESTAR
- LUCKY STARS
- MEGASTAR
- MOVIE STAR
- MUSTARD
- POLESTAR
- ROCK STAR
- STAR ANISE
- STAR MAP
- STAR FRUIT
- STAR POWER
- STAR-STUDDED
- STARBOARD
- STARBURST
- STARDOM
- STARDUST
- STARFISH
- STARGAZE
- STARLIGHT
- STARLING
- STARSHIP
- STARSTRUCK
- STARTUP
- STARVE
- SUPERSTAR
- WISH UPON A STAR

★	B	O	A	R	D	I	D	A	★	D	L	Y
E	T	H	G	I	L	★	★	S	H	I	P	P
D	T	S	N	S	U	P	E	R	★	O	A	T
O	★	L	U	C	K	Y	★	S	L	M	A	R
L	K	A	★	A	N	I	S	E	★	D	O	★
T	C	K	N	S	T	A	★	R	E	C	F	D
R	I	C	T	O	A	T	A	D	K	I	★	H
E	K	U	S	S	P	E	D	★	S	U	L	C
W	★	R	R	L	U	U	Z	H	M	I	M	★
O	L	T	U	F	T	D	H	A	T	E	S	N
P	I	S	B	S	★	A	★	S	G	V	M	R
★	N	★	★	★	D	O	M	A	I	★	E	O
T	G	M	O	V	I	E	★	E	O	W	R	C

TRIVIA QUESTION:

What is a shooting star?

Put the uncircled letters in order on the blanks.

It __ __ __ __ ' __ __ __ __ __ __ __ __ __

__ __ __. __ __ __ ' __ __ __ __ __ __ __ __ __ __ .

Full

The letters H-O-U-S-E are part of a ⌂ ful of words.
Use the clues to help figure out the rest of each word.

1. Ships look for this to find land: __ __ __ __ __ ⌂

2. Take care of a home when someone's out of town: ⌂ __ __ __

3. A toy with miniature furniture: __ __ __ __ ⌂

4. Where chickens live: __ __ __ ⌂

5. Indoor vegetation: ⌂ __ __ __ __ __

6. A place to learn: __ __ __ __ __ __ ⌂

7. Get hot drinks here: __ __ __ __ __ __ ⌂

8. Trials happen here: __ __ __ __ __ ⌂

9. A small insect with wings: ⌂ __ __ __

10. Has a barn nearby: __ __ __ __ ⌂

11. A place to play in a forest: __ __ __ __ ⌂

12. Type of party when someone moves in: ⌂ __ __ __ __ __ __

13. Plants grow here: __ __ __ __ __ ⌂

14. Where merchandise is stored: __ __ __ __ ⌂

Creeping Critters

> Every critter should only appear once in each row, column, and 2 x 3 box. Fill in the squares by drawing or writing the name of each critter.

Fruit Funnies

There are four fruit jokes on the next page. Use the emoji code to fill in the letters and finish the jokes. Then tell them to your friends!

Emoji Code

A   B   C   E

G   I   L   N

O   P   R   S

T   U   W   Y

Why did the orange go to the doctor?

_ _   _ _   _ _ _ _ _ _

_ _ _ _ _ _ _   _ _ _ _ .

What do you call a sad fruit?

_ _ _   _ _ _ _ _

What is an art teacher's favorite fruit?

_ _ _ _ _ _ _ _ _ _ _ _ _

What are bananas best at in gymnastics?

_ _ _ _ _ _

What is a twin's favorite fruit?

_ _ _ _ _

Follow Your

Circle sets of three emojis together that have one heart of each color. One side of each square must touch a side of another square in the same set. You are done when all the squares are circled.

Check 'Em Out

Can you complete each common phrase with the correct emoji?

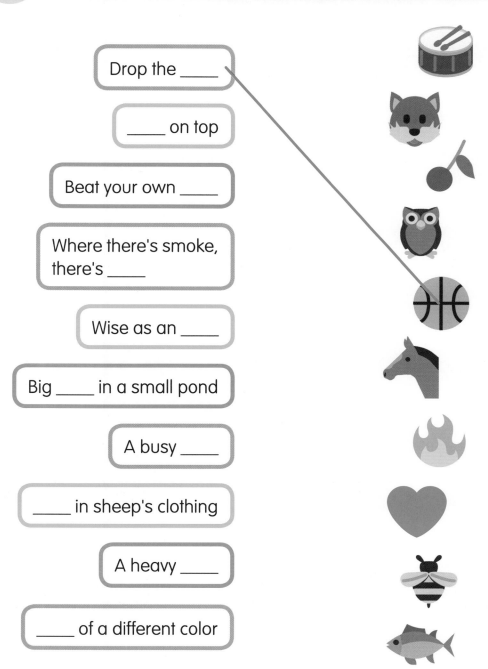

Drop the _____

_____ on top

Beat your own _____

Where there's smoke, there's _____

Wise as an _____

Big _____ in a small pond

A busy _____

_____ in sheep's clothing

A heavy _____

_____ of a different color

Nine-Lives Look

Each cat emoji but one appears nine times. Can you find the one that only appears eight times?

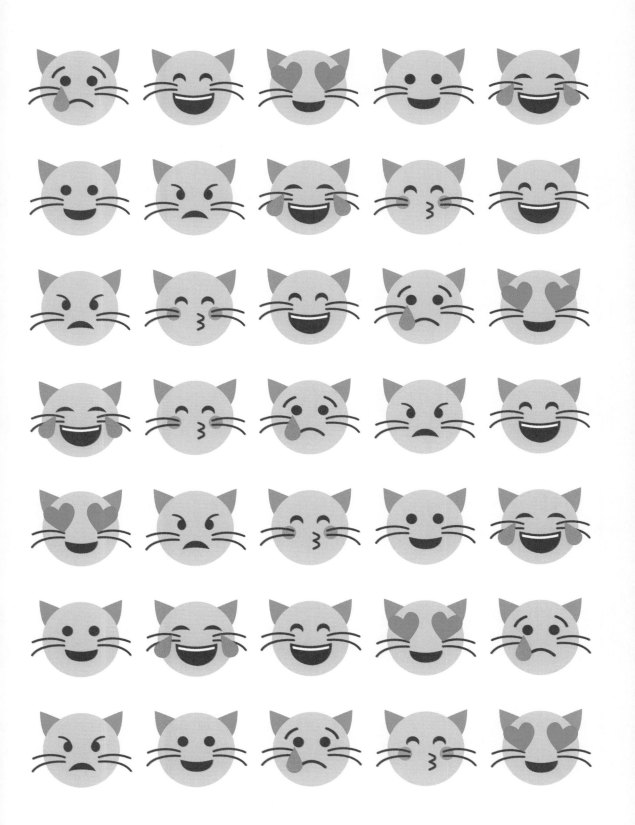

Best Emoji EVER

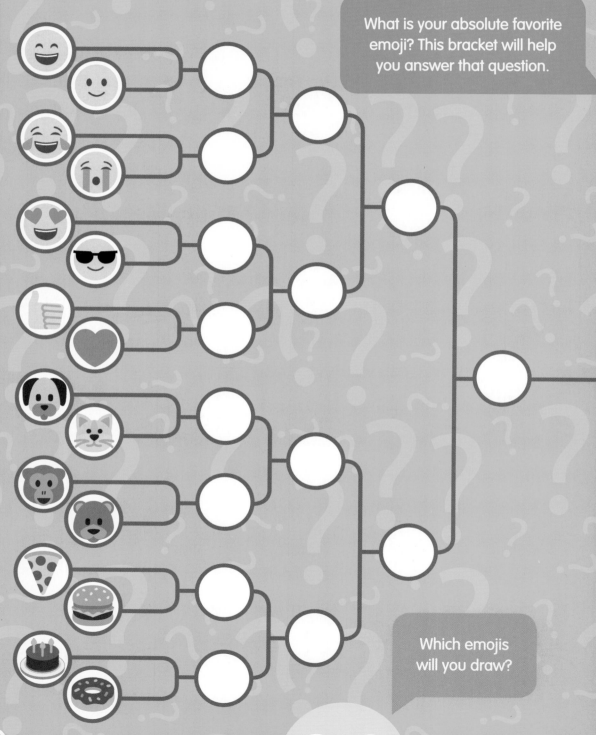

What is your absolute favorite emoji? This bracket will help you answer that question.

Which emojis will you draw?

Starting at the top, look at each pair of emojis and decide which you like the best. Draw the winner in the circle next to the pair. Then compare the next two emojis. Continue comparing until you come up with the best emoji ever— and put the sticker for that emoji on the trophy below.

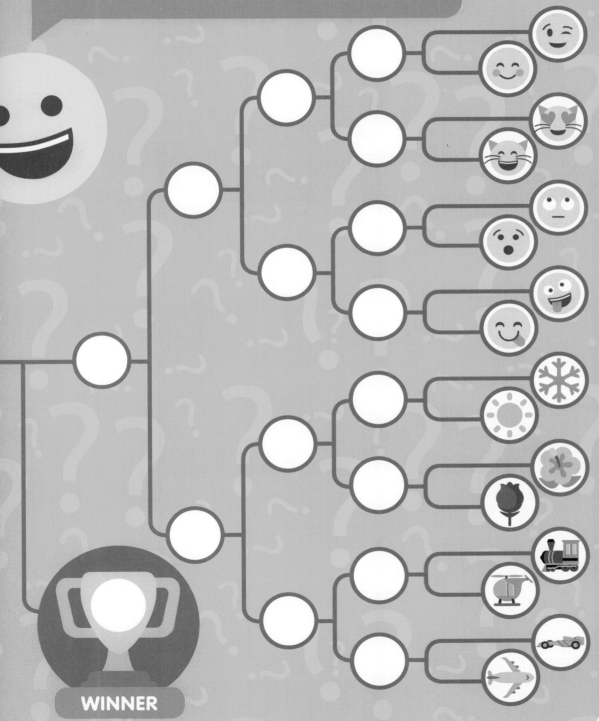

WINNER

87

ANSWERS

Pages 2-3

Page 4

Page 5

What do goldfish have in the back of their throat?
GOLDFISH HAVE TWO TEETH!

Page 6

1. CARD
2. CARVE
3. CARTON
4. CARPET
5. CARROT
6. CARTOON
7. CARIBOU
8. CARAMEL
9. CARDINAL
10. CARNIVAL
11. CARNATION
12. CARTWHEEL
13. CARNIVORE
14. CARSON CITY

Page 7

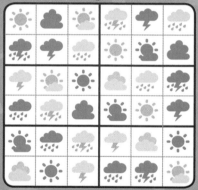

Pages 8-9

Where do horses go when they're sick?
TO THE HORSEPITAL

What does a bear call its grandfather?
GRAND-PAW

What dog can tell time?
A WATCH DOG

How does a hog write a letter?
WITH A PIGPEN

What kind of kitties like to go bowling?
ALLEY CATS

Page 10

Page 11

The **APPLE** of my eye 🍎
A couch **POTATO** 🥔
Don't cry over spilled **MILK** 🥛
One smart **COOKIE** 🍪
When life gives you **LEMONS** 🍋
Don't put all your **EGGS** in one basket 🥚🥚🥚
Bigger **FISH** to fry 🐟
The big **CHEESE** 🧀
Easy as **PIE** 🥧
Best thing since sliced **BREAD** 🍞

Pages 12-13

Page 14

Page 15

If the sun was the size of a door in your house, how big would the Earth be?
THE SIZE OF A NICKEL

Pages 16-17

Page 18

1. CONE
2. DONE
3. BONE
4. HONEY
5. MONEY
6. ALONE
7. SCONE
8. STONES
9. CYCLONE
10. PHONE
11. GONE
12. XYLOPHONE
13. THRONE
14. HONEST

Page 19

Pages 20-21

What do plants like to drink?
ROOT BEER

What plant loves math?
A SUM-FLOWER

What do you call a tree robber?
A LEAF THIEF

What did the big flower say to the little flower?
"HI, BUD."

What flower does everyone have?
TULIPS

ANSWERS

Page 22

🍿 = $8.00
🥨 = $6.00
🍭 = $3.00
🍫 = $5.00

Page 23

SKATE on thin ice ⛸️
Once in a blue MOON 🌑
Music to my EARS 👂
Like a kid in a CANDY store 🍬
As right as RAIN 🌧️
An open BOOK 📕
Every CLOUD has a silver lining ☁️
Sick as a DOG 🐶
The way the COOKIE crumbles 🍪
An early BIRD 🐦

Page 24

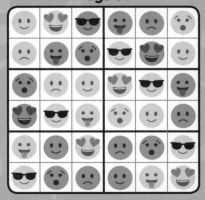

Page 25

1. sun + 🐟 = SUNFISH
2. back + ✋ = BACKHAND
3. 📕 + worm = BOOKWORM
4. 🔥 + place = FIREPLACE
5. green + 🏠 = GREENHOUSE
6. pop + 🌽 = POPCORN
7. wild + 🌼 = WILDFLOWER
8. ☀️ + glasses = SUNGLASSES
9. sweet + ❤️ = SWEETHEART
10. under + 🐶 = UNDERDOG

Pages 26-27

Page 28

Page 29

Why doesn't a bear wear socks?
HE PREFERS TO GO BAREFOOT.

Page 30

1. ACORN
2. CORNER
3. POPCORN
4. UNICORN
5. CORNFLAKES
6. CORNSTARCH
7. CORNEA
8. CORNET
9. PEPPERCORN
10. CORNBREAD
11. CORNUCOPIA
12. CORNY
13. CORNROWS
14. CORNMEAL

Page 31

Pages 32-33

Why did the cookie see a doctor?
IT FELT CRUMB-Y.

How do you make an egg roll?
YOU PUSH IT.

What did the mustard say during the race?
"TRY TO KETCHUP."

How do you fix a broken pizza?
WITH TOMATO PASTE

Page 34

Page 35

Hit the **BOOKS**
BIRDS of a feather
In the same **BOAT**
Play it by **EAR**
Change of **HEART**
Give someone a **HAND**
Don't cry **WOLF**
Get a **FOOT** in the door
I could eat a **HORSE**
Barking up the wrong **TREE**

Pages 36-37

Page 38

Page 39

The heart is an important organ in our bodies. It's also something else. What is it?
YOUR HEART IS ONE GIANT PUMP.

Pages 40-41

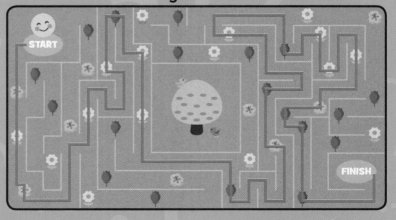

Page 42

1. GIANT
2. ELEPHANT
3. TENANT
4. ANTLER
5. ANTHEM
6. PENNANT
7. SERVANT
8. ANTENNA
9. PLEASANT
10. ANTIQUES
11. INFANT
12. PANTRY
13. MANTEL
14. HYDRANT

Page 43

Pages 44-45

What kind of music do mummies like?
WRAP

What is a bubble's least favorite type of music?
POP!

What does a skeleton use to make music?
A TROM-BONE

What do you get when a musician loses their beat?
A TEMPO-TANTRUM

Where do snowmen dance?
AT THE SNOWBALL

Page 46

Page 47

As white as **SNOW**
Over the **MOON**
Off on the wrong **FOOT**
That **SHIP** has sailed
On **CLOUD** nine
BUTTERFLIES in your stomach
Wear your **HEART** on your sleeve
TRAIN of thought
Fit as a **FIDDLE**
Add fuel to the **FIRE**

Page 48

Page 49

egg | shell | fish | sheep | dog | sled
ear | drum | stick | bird | house | boat
rain | water | melon | foot | note | book
pepper | corn | bread | gold | fish | bowl

Pages 50-51

Page 52

Page 53

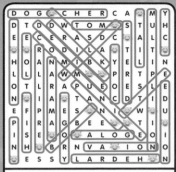

What taste are cats unable to detect?
CATS CAN'T TASTE SWEETNESS.

Page 54

1. YEAR
2. PEAR
3. EARN
4. CLEAR
5. EARTH
6. EARLY
7. LEARN
8. HEART
9. EARRING
10. FEARLESS
11. TEARDROPS
12. DISAPPEAR
13. UNDERWEAR
14. NEAR

Page 55

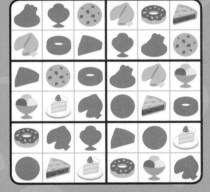

Pages 56-57

What did the mitt say to the baseball?
"CATCH YOU LATER."

What did the two strings do in the race?
THEY TIED.

Why did it get hot after the soccer game?
THE FANS LEFT.

What can you serve but not eat?
A TENNIS BALL

Why don't fish play basketball?
THEY'RE AFRAID OF THE NET.

Page 58

Page 59

Sly as a **FOX**
FISH out of water
Hold your **HORSES**
MONKEY business
A little **BIRD** told me
Let the **CAT** out of the bag
Night **OWL**
When **PIGS** fly
Can't teach an old **DOG** new tricks
Quiet as a **MOUSE**

ANSWERS

Pages 60-61

Page 62

Page 63

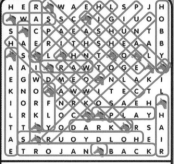

Why did the pony have to gargle?
**HE WAS JUST A
LITTLE HORSE.**

Pages 64-65

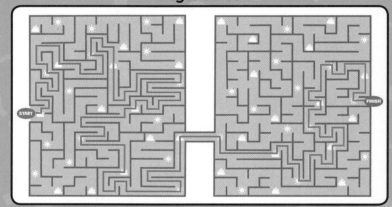

Page 66

1. CANOE
2. PECAN
3. CANVAS
4. CANDLE
5. VACANT
6. CANARY
7. TOUCAN
8. VOLCANO
9. HURRICANE
10. SCANNER
11. CANDY
12. CANOPY
13. CANINE
14. CANTALOUPE

Page 67

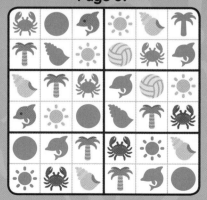

Pages 68-69

Why was the rabbit so happy?
SHE WAS A HOP-TIMIST.

How do clowns like their eggs?
FUNNY-SIDE UP

Why did Sandra cry on
February 29th?
IT WAS A WEEP YEAR.

Why was the dog sad?
HE HAD A RUFF DAY.

Page 70

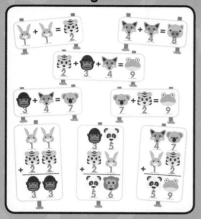

Page 71

'Til the **COWS** come home
Piece of **CAKE**
Head in the **CLOUDS**
Blind as a **BAT**
Take a **RAIN** check
Costs an **ARM** and a leg
FISH for a compliment
If the **SHOE** fits
CAT got your tongue
Comparing apples and **ORANGES**

Page 72

Page 73

1. 🦇 + boy = **BATBOY**
2. 🚚 + go = **CARGO**
3. 🥚 + shell = **EGGSHELL**
4. 🕷 + web = **SPIDERWEB**
5. friend + 🚢 = **FRIENDSHIP**
6. 🐴 + radish = **HORSERADISH**
7. 🌕 + light = **MOONLIGHT**
8. 👟 + lace = **SHOELACE**
9. 💪 + chair = **ARMCHAIR**
10. honey + 🐝 = **HONEYBEE**

Pages 74-75

Page 76

Page 77

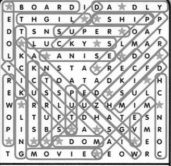

What is a shooting star?
It **ISN'T A STAR AT ALL.**
IT'S A METEOR.

Page 78

1. LIGHTHOUSE
2. HOUSESIT
3. DOLLHOUSE
4. HENHOUSE
5. HOUSEPLANT
6. SCHOOLHOUSE
7. COFFEEHOUSE
8. COURTHOUSE
9. HOUSEFLY
10. FARMHOUSE
11. TREEHOUSE
12. HOUSEWARMING
13. GREENHOUSE
14. WAREHOUSE

Page 79

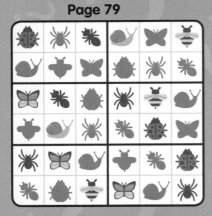

Pages 80-81

Why did the orange go to the doctor?
IT WASN'T PEELING WELL.

What do you call a sad fruit?
A BLUE BERRY

What is an art teacher's favorite fruit?
CRAYONBERRIES

What are bananas best at in gymnastics?
SPLITS

What is a twin's favorite fruit?
PEARS

Page 82

Page 83

Drop the **BALL**
CHERRY on top
Beat your own **DRUM**
Where there's smoke, there's **FIRE**
Wise as an **OWL**
Big **FISH** in a small pond
A busy **BEE**
WOLF in sheep's clothing
A heavy **HEART**
HORSE of a different color

Pages 84-85

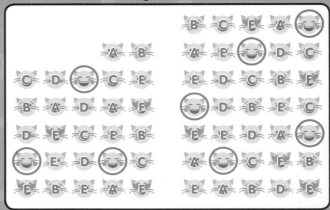

For information about permission to reprint selections from this book, please contact permissions@highlights.com.

Published by Highlights Press
815 Church Street
Honesdale, Pennsylvania 18431
ISBN: 978-1-68437-871-5
Manufactured in Dongguan, Guangdong, China
Mfg. 07/2019

First edition
Visit our website at Highlights.com.
10 9 8 7 6 5 4 3 2 1

Stick Together
Page 49
Use these stickers to make compound words.

 egg

 fish

 foot

 bird

 book

 pepper

 sheep

 ear

 sled

 gold

 rain

 boat

 bread

 bowl

 melon

 stick

Best Emoji Ever
Pages 86–87
Which emoji won your bracket? Put the winning sticker on the trophy on page 87.
Use the rest for emoji sticker fun!

7871-01

Emoji-fy your world with the BONUS stickers below and on the next page.